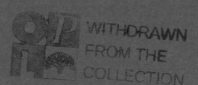

EXCAVATING THE PAST

ANCIENT CHINA

Jane Shuter

Heinemann Library
Chicago, Illinois

© 2006 Heinemann Library
a division of Reed Elsevier Inc.
Chicago, Illinois

Customer Service 888–454–2279

Visit our website at
www.heinemannraintree.com

Photo research by Maria Joannou and Catherine
Bevan
Designed by Richard Parker and Tinstar Design
Ltd (www.tinstar.co.uk)
Printed in China by WKT Company Limited

10 09 08 07 06
10 9 8 7 6 5 4 3 2

**Library of Congress Cataloging-in-
Publication Data**

Shuter, Jane.
   Ancient China / Jane Shuter.
      p. cm. — (Excavating the past)
   Audience: Ages 9-11.
   Audience: Grades 4-6.
   Includes bibliographical references and index.
   ISBN 1-4034-5995-9 (library binding -
hardcover)
   1. China—Civilization—To 221 B.C.—Juvenile
literature. 2. China—Civilization—221 B.C.-960
A.D.—Juvenile literature. 3. China—
Antiquities—Juvenile literature. 4. Excavations
(Archaeology)—China—Juvenile literature. I.
Title. II. Series.
   DS741.65.S57 2006
   931—dc22   2005009178

Acknowledgments
The publishers would like to thank the following
for permission to reproduce photographs: Ancient
Art & Architecture pp. **12** (R.Kawka), **15** (Dr. S.
Coyne), **17** (Uniphoto/Ancient Art & Architecture
Collection), **18** bottom (R Sheridan), **25, 42**
(Uniphoto Press Japan); Art Resource pp. **11, 14**
(Bildarchiv Preussischer Kulturbesitz/Petra
Stuening); Arthur M Sackler Gallery archives p. **6**
both (Smithsonian Museum); British Museum p. **9**;
China Pictorial p. **34**; Corbis pp. **7** (Royal Ontario
Museum), **10** (Lowell Georgia), **19** (Asian Art &
Archaeology, Inc), **30** (Todd Gipstein), **38** (Jeffery
Newbury), **39** (Royal Ontario Museum), **43**
(Charles O'Rear); Cultural Relics Publishing House
pp. **8, 9**; DK Images pp. **24, 41**; Getty Images pp.
13 (Photodisc), **35**; Harcourt Education Ltd p. **16**
(Debbie Rowe); Jane & Paul Shuter p. **32** both;
Jingzhou Regional Museum pp. **21, 33**; Natural
History Museum p. **5**; Nelson-Stkins Museum of
Art p. **29** (Kansas City/Robert Newcombe); Picture
Desk p. **22** (The Art Archive/ Freer Gallery of
Art); Science & Society Picture Library p. **40**; The
Palace Museum, Beijing p. **36**; Werner Forman
Archive pp. **18** top, **28**.

Cover photograph of the Great Wall of China
reproduced with permission of Getty Images
(Taxi/Travel Pix.) Small picture of terracotta figure
reproduced with permission of Art Archive (Musée
Cernuschi Paris/Dagli Orti.)

Illustrations by Jeff Edwards and Eikon Illustration.

The publishers would like to thank Dr. Gwen
Bennett of Washington University for her
assistance in the preparation of this book.

Every effort has been made to contact
copyright holders of any material reproduced in
this book. Any omissions will be rectified in
subsequent printings if notice is given to the
publishers.

CONTENTS

Dates B.C.E. **and** C.E.

B.C.E. after a date means "before the common era." The years count down to 0.

C.E. before a date stands for "of the common era." It means that the year is counted from after the year 0.

ARCHAEOLOGY AND ANCIENT CHINA

China is huge, about 9.5 million square miles (15 million square kilometers). It is so big that different areas have very different climates. They range from cold, dry deserts to hot, humid rain forests. China has a long history that archaeologists are still uncovering. In 1994 they discovered bones that showed people lived just south of the Yangzi River about 2 million years ago. In about 2000 B.C.E. the first kingdoms grew up. These were larger areas controlled by one ruling family, called a dynasty. The Ancient Chinese period begins with these kingdoms.

The Ancient Chinese

The Ancient Chinese period runs from the first kingdom ruled by a single dynasty to the takeover of China by invading Mongols in C.E. 1279. The first Ancient Chinese kingdom was much smaller than modern China. It grew over time to be almost the same size.

▷ *This map shows modern China and the smallest and biggest empires of Ancient China.*

Map legend:
- Xia Kingdom
- Shang Kingdom
- Qin Kingdom
- Modern China

N

RUSSIA
KAZAKSTAN
MONGOLIA
KOREA
KYRGYZSTAN
CHINA
Dunhang
Anyang
Xian
Erlitou
NEPAL
BHUTAN
INDIA
BANGLADESH
MYANMAR
VIETNAM
LAOS

| 0 | 500 miles |
| 0 | 1000 km |

How early Chinese people lived

Archaeologists have discovered that early Chinese people lived in small villages of about 300 people living in 50–100 houses. These people lived in large family groups, called clans, who were supposed to share the same ancestors, far back in the past. Small villages of up to 50 houses usually had only one clan. Bigger villages had two or three clans. The early Chinese farmed, fished, and kept animals. Archaeologists know that people had different ways of life in different parts of China, and did not see themselves as Chinese. When archaeologists talk about the early Chinese people they identify them by the different kinds of pottery styles they used. People that share a pottery style are seen as connected, possibly through clan marriages.

From about 2500 B.C.E., some villages were built with earth walls around them. Only a few of these villages have been found. It is hard to understand why some villages changed without more evidence. However some archaeologists think they show that villagers were fighting each other more often, trying to take more land. If they were fighting regularly, they needed a wall for protection.

△ *This is a reconstruction of what the whole skull of a person archaeologists named "Peking Man" looked like when alive about 500,000 years ago. Bones from over 40 different people were found between 1921 and 1935.*

WHO WAS Carl Whiting Bishop?

Carl Whiting Bishop was an American, born in Tokyo in 1881. He was sent to school in the United States, and studied anthropology at Columbia University. He went to work for the Freer Gallery of Art in Washington in 1922 and led their archaeological expeditions to China until 1934. He insisted on careful excavation and record keeping. He died in 1942.

Early archaeology

Explorers from the West had been finding their way to China along a trade route called the Silk Road since medieval times. They took away with them many treasures from China's past, dug up and sold by local people. However, the rush of European archaeologists began in the early 1900s. In 1907 a British archaeologist, Aurel Stein, discovered many valuable silk scrolls and took them back to the British Museum. There was a sudden push to find more treasures, mostly by Europeans and Americans looking for beautiful artifacts. They did not all try to sell them to make money. Most took the artifacts back to museums, to be both studied and admired. Several of them actually worked for museums. Most early archaeologists were also careful with their work and kept detailed records of their findings.

▷ Workers used baskets to remove the dirt that was cleared during early excavations.

Changing the rules

In 1949 the People's Republic of China was set up. It did not welcome foreigners, but it did see the importance of archaeology. The government made strict rules about taking artifacts out of China and letting foreign archaeologists in. It also made archaeology, like most other things in China, state-run. The government was not interested in finding spectacular graves. It was more interested in understanding the lives of ordinary people in the past. The government gave Chinese archaeologists money to excavate sites, but they could only excavate where the government gave them permission.

Archaeology Challenge

Archaeologists excavate carefully, layer by layer. This is because each layer represents a different period of time. This is called stratigraphy. Archaeologists mark out the site in grids and keep careful records—written, drawn and, if possible, photographic, too. In this way they build up a picture of how life on the site they are excavating changed over time.

Development and archaeology

In the 1950s the government built a lot of new factories, new towns, huge communal farms, roads, and dams. All of these projects involved digging up the land, and many new tombs, graves, and other sites were found. In 1953 the government allowed work to stop in Xinglong, in Hebei Province, while archaeologists uncovered an iron-making factory from the Warring States period.

△ *This jade carving was made to be placed in a grave about 5,000 years ago.*

EMERGING KINGDOMS

Early archaeologists had no evidence that the first kingdom the ancient Chinese talked about, the Xia (around 2205 B.C.E. to 1700 B.C.E.), really existed. Then, in 1959, archaeologists found an ancient city at Erlitou. It was where ancient historians said the Xia ruled and it dated from about 2000 B.C.E., about the right time. But archaeologists argue over whether it is a Xia city, or just an early Shang one—the Shang were the next ruling dynasty. Whoever ruled Erlitou, it is one of the earliest ancient Chinese city discovered so far.

What makes a kingdom?

Ancient Chinese kingdoms were different from earlier settlements. They covered a larger area with many clan groups, all obeying one ruler. This ruler lived in a palace, far grander than any other house, in a capital city. People ran different parts of his kingdom for him, in return for land and power. Earlier clan groups had sometimes traded and sometimes fought, but mostly they kept to themselves. The new, larger, kingdoms took more notice of each other. They traded more. Archaeologists know this, because they have made a careful study of trade goods. Ancient kingdoms also fought more. Their rulers were constantly trying to take more land.

Fantasy or Fact?

Archaeologists used to say the first Chinese kingdoms were in central and northern China. Then, in 1986, some brick-makers, digging for clay, found a sacrificial pit at Sanxingdui, about 600 miles (960 kilometers) south of Anyang, the biggest Shang city. They found a rich burial, showing there was a southern kingdom as powerful as the Shang.

△ *This bronze figure was found at Sanxingdui in 1986.*

"Wearing goggles to keep out the dust, in a tearing gale that threatens to fling you to the bottom of 30-foot deep pits is not easy. Nor is supervising the workers and keeping the detailed records that a scientific archaeologist needs."

Herrlee Creel, an American archaeologist talking about a visit to Anyang in 1930.

The Shang

The Shang ruled China after the Xia. Their last capital was Anyang, on the Huan River, north of the Yellow River. We know a lot about Anyang because archaeologists have been working there since 1928.

△ *Shang bronzeworkers made the design in clay, then made molds of all the parts of the design and joined them together. They then poured bronze into the mold.*

Rich and poor

Anyang shows people in ancient kingdoms did not all live and work together. Anyang had a section for ordinary people, with workshops and homes, and a section for the rich, with much larger homes. There was a section for the royal family, with palaces, temples, and workshops. Each section had its own burial areas. The workshops show there were specialist bronze workers, potters, and jewelers. The Shang are famous for the huge bronze containers covered with complicated designs found in Shang graves.

A queen's cup

This ivory and turquoise beaker from the Shang period was found in the tomb of Fu Hao, wife of the Shang ruler Wu Ding. There were elephants in some parts of China at the time, so ivory could be found in China, but the turquoise must have been brought from far away by a trader.

DID YOU KNOW? Early kingdoms sometimes went on trading even when at war with each other!

9

An accidental discovery

In 1899 a student of Chinese writing, Liu Tieyun, visited a sick friend, Wang Yirong. Chinese patients have to grind up and boil their own medicine. Wang's medicine included some tortoise shell and Liu saw writing on it. The medicine seller could not say exactly where the shell came from, but said bones from the same place also sometimes had writing on them. Liu and Wang collected shells and bones, and published a book of the writings in 1903.

Using the bones

The historian Luo Zhenyu is said to have locked himself in his room for 40 days until he had worked out how oracle bones were used. He discovered that the Shang kings wrote a question on one side of the bone (usually an animal's wide, flat shoulder bone) or shell. He might ask about his own health or whether his unborn child would be male. But the kings mostly asked about war or running the country. One or more small pieces were drilled out. A heated point was pushed into the hole, making the bone or shell crack, being careful not to split the bone or shell into pieces. The question was written and the way the cracks ran then gave the answer to the question.

△ *The answers to the questions on oracle bones like this could only be worked out by priests.*

WHO WAS Sun Yirang?

Sun Yirang was born in 1848 and became an expert in the Chinese language and its development. He studied the writings on shells and bones. He translated them and published a book saying that they were "oracle bones," used by the Shang kings to ask questions about the future. He died in 1908.

Writing spreads

Writing was an important skill in ancient China. Rulers sent messages around their kingdom. The officials who ran the kingdom kept written records of work done and food given out. Early records were kept on strips of bamboo. Archaeologists found a collection of these in a tomb robbed in about C.E. 250. There would have been many more, but the robbers had grabbed handfuls and lit them to use as torches while they looted the tomb.

The Zhou

The Zhou fought and defeated the Shang in about 1050 B.C.E. They then set out to capture more and more of China, and their kingdom was eventually about twice the size of the Shang kingdom. The Zhou had to fight to keep control of China. In 475 B.C.E. the kingdom divided and many different states formed. They fought each other almost constantly, so this time is called the Warring States period. Slowly, larger states swallowed smaller ones until there were just seven at war with each other. By 221 B.C.E. the ruler of Qin had defeated all his enemies and united China.

Painted lacquer

This clothes chest is typical of the beautiful chests made for the rich rulers of the kingdom. The chest is covered in lacquer and decorated with detailed pictures. Lacquer is a tree sap that can be dyed and used like paint or varnish. When it dries it is heat resistant, water resistant, and very shiny. It is painted on layer by layer. The more layers there are the more complicated the designs can be.

ONE

When the Qin took over China in 221 B.C.E. their leader, Zheng, renamed himself Shihuangdi—the First Emperor. He made it clear that, for him, China was beginning again. He did not respect scholars or their books and banned the teachings of the thinker Confucius because they respected age, experience, and the past. He made everyone in China use the same money, the same weights and measures, and even the same size of cart. This improved transportation and communication across the region.

A new way of ruling

The First Emperor did not want to rule China by giving the lords of different states power to rule for him. Even if they had not fought him during the Warring States period, they might try to take power in the future. So he took away their lands and made them move to his capital city, Xianyang. He divided China into 36 areas. Each area had a military leader, someone to run day-to-day life, and an inspector who checked up on the others and reported to the First Emperor. They were not lords, but less important people, chosen by the First Emperor to be loyal to him.

Fantasy or Fact?

An ancient history book, written during the Han Dynasty, said that the First Emperor made all of the lords he brought to Xianyang live in palaces along the cliffs overlooking the Wei River. At first there was no evidence for this, but archaeologists excavating along the cliffs have now found 27 different large buildings that could be palaces. Two have tiles decorated with the symbols of two kingdoms the Emperor took over.

▷ *The hole in the middle of these ancient Chinese coins meant they could be threaded onto a string and tied securely to the body.*

EYEWITNESS

"The land was divided, battles broke out daily, blood flowed over the Plain. Now our emperor has made the world [China] one family and weapons are put aside."

From the beginning of a legal document from the time of the First Emperor.

Fantasy or Fact?

People used to think that the earliest Great Wall was built entirely during the reign of the First Emperor. Archaeologists have studied the earliest parts of the wall and found that they date back to the Warring States period, although it was the First Emperor who had them joined up to make a single wall.

A tyrant?

Under the First Emperor there were many laws. The punishments for breaking them were harsh. A person could be executed or sent to work on the Great Wall until they dropped dead if they were found to own a book by Confucius. However, cities and farmland were not being destroyed by war. This was something he always reminded people of if he thought a new law would be unpopular.

The Great Wall

The Great Wall would run for 1,678 miles (2,700 kilometers) if it ran straight. However, it makes big loops and there are some places that have up to three extra walls. The workers actually built nearly 6,214 miles (10,000 kilometers) of wall from earth rammed down hard in layers with pebbles, reeds, or wood. So many died (some estimates say one person for every few feet of wall built) that it has been called "the longest graveyard in the world."

DID YOU KNOW? Elephants were used to do some of the heavy lifting on the Great Wall.

Writing it down

The people of China spoke many different languages when the First Emperor took over. They had different written languages, too, all based on "characters" that grew out of picture writing. The First Emperor made everyone use the same written language with only 3,000 characters. It was used for everything from laws made by the Emperor to shopping lists made in towns far from the capital city. The ancient Chinese, like many early peoples, did not just use writing for letters, official documents, and lists. Archaeologists have found writing on many other things, too. Some Shang bronzes have writing on them, as well as beautiful designs. The weights and measures from the time of the First Emperor have the First Emperor's law about making weights and measures the same written on them.

▷ *This bronze Shang axe head has writing along its edges. It was found in a tomb and may have been used to execute the servants who were to be buried with their dead master to work for him in the afterlife.*

WHO WAS Li Si?

Li Si moved to the state of Qin in 247 B.C.E., during the Warring States period. He became a close advisor of the First Emperor. It was on his advice that the First Emperor made everyone use the same written language and banned and burned many writings from before 221 B.C.E. because "they confuse and excite the ordinary people." Li Si was executed by the Second Emperor in 208 B.C.E.

WHO WAS Sima Qian?

Sima Qian was born in 145 B.C.E. and worked for the Han Dynasty rulers as a historian and scholar, as his father had before him. The Han took over from the Qin. Sima Qian wrote Records of the Historian. He studied as many artifacts and written documents from the time as he could. He died in 85 B.C.E..

A dramatic end

Archaeologists sometimes use written documents from the past to help them find towns or burial places. One of these, *Records of the Historian*, is a history of China written in about C.E. 170 by Sima Qian for the Han rulers who followed the Qin. Qian is often accurate, for instance the First Emperor's tomb is where he said it was, and he tells of his dramatic death.

The First Emperor died suddenly on a journey around China. Li Si, his advisor, wanted to replace Prince Fusu, who was to rule next, with another son, Huhai. So he acted as if the Emperor was alive. This was easy, as the Emperor disliked being seen. He traveled in a litter. Li Si took food to the Emperor and gave out his orders as usual. One order was to Fusu, saying he was a bad son, and was to kill himself. Fusu, suspecting nothing, did so. The next order made Huhai the next to rule. By this time the summer heat was making the body of the Emperor smell horrible. Li Si ordered a cart full of fish to travel next to the First Emperor's litter. This stopped anyone suspecting he was dead until Huhai could announce his father's sudden death and take over as Second Emperor.

▷ *This is the First Emperor, Shihuangdi, in terrocotta.*

WEAPONS AND WARFARE

On March 29, 1974, farmers from Xiyang village were drilling a well for water and found pieces of terracotta and some bronze weapons. The government sent archaeologists to the site, about a mile (1.5 kilometers) from the First Emperor's tomb, where they discovered a huge pit mainly full of life-sized terracotta warriors. It was an army built to guard the Emperor in death. Archaeologists have worked on the site since 1974. They can now tell us a lot about the First Emperor's warriors, including their weapons, how they were organized, and even the color of their uniforms.

Organization

All ancient Chinese rulers needed an army. The Han Dynasty, which followed the Qin, was the first to have a full-time army of trained soldiers. Before this, ordinary soldiers were conscripts, farmers and workers made to fight, not trained soldiers. The First Emperor's army had officers and ordinary soldiers that wore different armor and carried different weapons. The most important officers are larger than life size, to stand out from the ordinary soldiers. The army had foot soldiers, cavalry, archers, and charioteers on horses.

▷ *Here are just a few of the terracotta warriors.*

16

△ *Some of the weapons belonging to the terracotta warriors have become embedded in rock. They have had to be excavated very carefully.*

Weapons

Archaeologists have analyzed the metals of the weapons the warriors carried. Weapons were made from a mixture of copper, tin, and lead. The foot soldiers carried long spears, with sharp heads. Their officers carried swords. They were also coated with a thin layer of chrome to prevent rust. The archers carried wooden crossbows with metal arrows. Many warriors carried daggers.

Armor

Armor keeps a soldier safe, but weighs him down the more he wears. Armor was made by overlapping pieces of iron or leather, tied with silk, sometimes with iron studs, too. Armor varied, partly by job (cavalry wore wide robes for riding and a tight-fitting helmet for falls) and partly by importance (officers wore more armor). Robes or trousers and tunics were made in green, red, purple, blue, and black.

Fighting

The warriors in the main pit were arranged in correct fighting formation. An army would have archers in front, firing their arrows up to 2,600 feet (800 meters). As the army moved forward, they stayed back, firing from a distance. Behind them came the fast-moving chariots pulled by four horses. Behind these came the foot soldiers and their officers. They fought with the enemy hand-to-hand, after the archers and the charioteers had done as much damage as they could. To the sides of the main army were groups of archers and cavalry, who attacked the enemy wherever they were needed.

DID YOU KNOW? The terracotta army's weapons were still sharp when they were excavated in 1974.

BELIEFS AND BURIALS

The ancient Chinese had a complicated system of beliefs. The earliest Chinese believed in many spirits and demons that affected their daily lives. They also prayed to the spirits of their ancestors, because they believed people went to an afterlife when they died, where they could make things happen in the world of the living.

Ways of living

The ancient Chinese believed that the way they behaved was important. Three different teachers wrote about how living a good life would make that life better and make sure your afterlife was good, too. Two of these, Lao Tzu and Confucius, lived in about 450 B.C.E. The third was Buddha. His religion, Buddhism, came to China from India along the Silk Road trade route during the rule of the Han. Most Chinese people followed the teachings of one of these thinkers.

△ *Some of the earliest Buddhist images were made in the Yungang Caves. They can still be visited today.*

WHO WAS Confucius?

Confucius was born in about 551 B.C.E. His parents died when he was young, but he managed to learn enough to work first as an official, then as a teacher. His thinking concentrated on people and how they should behave toward each other, while Daoism stressed that people were part of one universe in which everything was related. Both stressed the need for harmony. Confucius died in 479 B.C.E.

EYEWITNESS

"The young should be obedient at home, well behaved in public, truthful, and attentive. They should love their friends and treat everyone with goodwill."

From the teachings of Confucius.

Temples, monks, and special places

Followers of Daoism worshipped at small stone shrines set up in places that had special natural beauty. This was to help them meditate, to feel part of the beauty around them. Buddhists did this too, but they also built bigger, spectacularly decorated places to worship in. Archaeologists have discovered many carvings of the Buddha in caves and temples. Some are brightly colored, some huge, but plain. They have discovered that monks lived at some of these temples. Monks spent all their time studying the teachings of Buddha and caring for the special sites and the valuable scrolls with the teachings of Buddha written on. It was the discovery by Aurel Stein of some of these scrolls, in caves at Dunhuang in 1907, that led to the rush of European and American archaeologists traveling to China.

▷ *Inscribed bronze vessels, like this one dating back to the Shang Dynasty, may have been used to decorate Buddhist temples.*

Death and burial

The ancient Chinese believed in a life after death. They believed that people in this afterlife would need their bodies, food, drink, servants, and all their possessions. So they took care to preserve the bodies of the dead, and buried them with everything they would need for the afterlife. This means that when archaeologists find a tomb they also find many things that tell them about everyday life in China at the time the person was buried. The richer and more important the person was, the more possessions they were buried with. Even the poor were often given a string of beads, a loaf of bread, and a pottery bowl.

Tombs tell all?

Unfortunately the ancient Chinese knew that rich people were buried with valuable possessions. Many tombs that archaeologists find were looted in ancient times, or later, by people hoping to make money by selling these possessions. This changed when the Chinese government began to reward people for pointing out local sites, and punished them if they were caught treasure hunting.

Archaeology Challenge

Forensic scientists study the bodies of the dead. When they examine an ancient body, they can tell a great deal about the dead person. When they examined the Lady Xin, who died in about 165 B.C.E., they discovered that she had been just 5 feet (1.5 meters) tall. She was about 50 years old when she died, and overweight. She had taken too little exercise, so her arteries had narrowed and this gave her heart problems. She eventually died of a heart attack.

常毋乗福羊卯其天有常毋乗福羊卯其

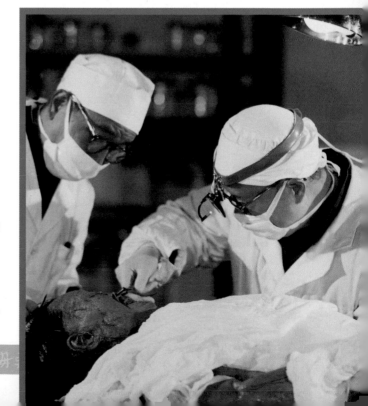

▷ *A forensic scientist prepares the Lady Xin for an examination in 1973.*

Suits of jade

In 1968 archaeologists were called when what looked like the entrance to a tomb was found on Mount Ling, southwest of Beijing. This tomb had not been broken into. It was sealed off by two brick walls with a layer of iron poured between them, and the corridor behind it was filled with rock. All this had been done to protect the bodies of Liu Sheng, son of a Han emperor, and one of his wives, Dou Wan. They had both been buried in suits made of thousands of pieces of jade fixed together with gold wire. A skilled worker would have taken at least ten years to make just one of these. Jade was thought to preserve the bodies of the dead. The tomb was also full of possessions.

EYEWITNESS

"When the emperor died his body was wrapped in twelve layers of reddish yellow silk. A suit was made for him, out of jade. It had the shape of armor and the pieces were stitched up with gold thread."

Written about the burial of an early Han emperor by the writer Wei Hong. People knew that jade burial suits were supposed to exist, but there was no evidence until Liu Sheng's burial was found.

Serving the dead

Until the time of the First Emperor real servants of important masters were killed and buried with their master upon his death. After this people were buried with models of servants. The models were usually small and made from pottery or wood. However, the First Emperor had life-size warriors, acrobats, and officials made for his burial. These models come from Jingzhou.

LIVES OF THE POOR

Poor people in Ancient China did the most difficult, dangerous, and unpleasant work. They were paid the least and lived in the worst conditions. The most important ancient Chinese were also the richest and saw the poor as unimportant. They understood that farming and providing food were some of the most vital jobs in China, but they did not treat farmers well. Archaeologists have found few remains of the lives of the poor.

Farmers

Most people in Ancient China were farmers. The crops they grew depended on the part of China they lived in. In the warm, wet south, rice was the most important food. Rice could not grow in the north, so farmers grew grains like wheat, barley, and millet instead. Until the rule of the First Emperor, farmers did not own their land. They worked for the lord who owned the land they were born and raised on, and could not move away. They had to give the lord all their crops. If he told them to move to a different part of his lands, they had to go. They had to fight when he told them to. In return the lord had to give them a home, food, and clothing. From the time of the First Emperor farmers had more freedom. They could move, they could own land (if they could afford to buy it), and the lord paid them to work.

Timeless work

This painting of farmers and their families harvesting rice was painted just after the end of the period we call Ancient China. However, scenes like families collecting rice by hand, watched by the lord's official, had happened in the same way for the previous 2,000 years. Some farmers in poorer districts were still using wooden digging sticks and stone tools.

△ *This is an artist's drawing of a farming village.*

Village life

Farmers lived in small groups, often from the same clan, in villages. It made farming more efficient. The biggest village in an area was where the local lord lived. This was the place where people came regularly to bring food to the lord, and to trade any food left over among themselves. Many villages had a wall around them, to keep the farm animals in and to keep wild animals out.

EYEWITNESS

"Cutting stalks at noontime, sweat falls to the earth. Remember, each grain of rice in your bowl comes from such hardship."

Said by the ancient Chinese philosopher Cheng Chang-Pao.

Homes

Each farmer and his family lived in a one-room house, sometimes with a shed on the side for their animals. The size and shape of the houses varied, as did what they were made from. It depended on whether wood, stone, or just clay could be collected near by. Most farmers had a few chickens and maybe a pig. Very few of them could afford to have a horse or an ox, useful for plowing at planting time. Often several villagers owned and shared one of these animals.

Poor people in towns

The poor in the town lived crammed together, often with several families living in one room. The men went out to work, often doing the heavy work for craft workers. They beat the air out of the clay and stoked the fire for potters. They stoked the fire or melted down scraps of metal to be reused for the metalworkers. Older men fetched and carried, and the oldest swept the workshops or streets. Women looked for work in the jobs that poorer women were allowed to do, such as making silk, working in a laundry, or cleaning.

Working for the emperor

No matter what work poor people did, the emperor could take them away from their homes and families to work on big building works, such as the Great Wall, or to fight in the army. Even when the Han made the army a full-time job, workers were wanted as ordinary foot soldiers in times of war. Sometimes a poor man lost his job and could not find another. If no one in the family could find work, the father sometimes sold himself into slavery to get some money for his family.

▷*Archaeologists have found many examples of the colorful silk clothes of the rich. Far fewer clothes of poor people have survived.*

WHO WERE the people in the mass graves?

The emperor's officials who organized tomb, road, canal, and wall building placed little value on the lives of the workers. If a lot of them died, the officials just sent for more. However, archaeologists have found that in many large burials of workers, someone threw in a piece of broken tile or pot with the name of the dead person and where they came from. Most of them, even though they were young, had bodies that were badly worn and damaged by the work they had to do.

Always hungry

Poor people in ancient China were always hungry. They seldom had enough to eat, mostly boiled rice or grain made into porridge, depending on where they lived. Poor farmers were usually better off than poor people in towns. They were more likely to be able to grow some food of their own, as well as food for the lord, so they could have vegetables as well as rice or porridge. They could also fish or hunt wild animals. On the other hand, the poor in towns had a better chance of making money by begging on the streets, or by finding someone who wanted a letter delivered, or some other small errand done.

EYEWITNESS

"Even the most efficient housewife cannot cook a meal without rice."

An ancient Chinese proverb.

Slaves

The huge building works of the First Emperor would have been impossible without gangs of slaves. Slaves were either criminals, people who sold themselves into slavery, or people who had been captured in war. They were rarely set free.

◁ *This square was built to commemorate the First Emperor.*

DID YOU KNOW? Poor people in north China did not eat rice, as it had to be traded from the south.

LIVES OF SKILLED WORKERS

In Ancient China, farmers were seen as more important than skilled workers. However, many skilled workers had a better life. These were the workers who could make things from bronze or iron, or make pottery, jewelry, or embroidered silks. Most skilled workers and their families lived in towns, where they could set up workshops. Some workers worked outside towns, like the ironworkers who worked in foundries near where the iron was mined from the ground.

Who did they work for?

Many skilled workers worked for themselves. Some workshops were small enough for a father and his sons to run it without needing to pay extra workers. There were some important industries, such as making iron and making salt, that only people who worked for the emperor could do. So all ironworkers worked for the emperor and were paid with food or money. Ancient Chinese ironworkers were very skilled. Archaeologists have found an iron foundry that was making steel during the reign of the First Emperor. Steel was not made in Europe until the 1700s.

Just one bowl

Archaeologists found a lacquered bowl in a Han burial that showed just how much work went into a single object made in a workshop and how many people could be involved. The writing on the bottom of this bowl said: "Sized by Jin, lacquered by Ji, final coat by [name unreadable], handles gilded by [name unreadable], painted by Li, engraved by Yi, cleaned and polished by Zheng, checked by Yi, guarded by Zhang, overseen by Liang and his assistant Feng, written by Bao."

▷ *Ancient Chinese towns were very busy places.*

What were towns like?

Archaeologists have found several ancient Chinese cities. They were carefully built with a wall all around and streets running in a criss-cross grid pattern. There were different areas for the skilled workers, officials and, if it was a capital city, a special walled area for the emperor and

△ *This is an artist's drawing of an ancient Chinese courtyard house.*

the people who lived with him, called his court. There were open spaces for markets, and there were parks. Local officials ran the markets. Smaller towns were less well planned. They were also walled, with at least one open space for markets.

Where did the workers live?

Very few ancient Chinese homes of any kind have survived for archaeologists to study. The Chinese preferred building with wood to building with stone. This meant homes were less likely to survive. The poorest skilled workers had a small courtyard, with three or four rooms leading off it and a separate kitchen. The better off the workers were, the bigger their courtyard and rooms. Some even had a second floor to their houses.

DID YOU KNOW? Many parts of China had earthquakes, so houses often had to be rebuilt. **27**

FAMILY LIFE

The earliest Chinese people lived in large family clan groups and many people in ancient Chinese villages were still part of the same clan. Most Chinese people had their marriages arranged by their parents, and a wife left her family to live with her husband's family. Having lots of children was seen as a blessing, especially if they were boys. Archaeologists have found many artifacts that show pictures of families and emphasize the importance of family life. A silk painting, left at a Buddhist shrine in C.E. 983, includes a prayer asking that: "there may be many children and grandchildren, for ten thousand years."

Archaeology Challenge

Archaeologists try to find out as much as they can about artifacts from X-rays and scans. These are useful for showing, for instance, the places where decorated bronze pots are joined, to work out how they were made. Bodies from tombs can be examined this way, too, without the need to cut them open.

Women at work

Most wealthy women did not go out to work. They were expected to stay at home and look after the house and the family. Most rich families had at least one servant who did all the hard cleaning and cooking work.

Tea

Tea was an important drink in China. Everyone drank tea, although poor people drank it very weak and often used the leaves over and over again. The Chinese grew their own tea, but also traded tea in from India. Indian tea was stronger and more bitter, and also more expensive. It was stored in jars, like this one.

Officials

From the First Emperor on, emperors ran China by using a lot of officials, rather than lords and the people the lords ruled. There were many different kinds of officials. Those who were in charge of large areas of China were rich and powerful. They did not really do any of the hard work of running their area, although they were the ones who the emperor would blame if anything went wrong. They had hundreds of less important officials working for them, in the town and in the countryside. Many of these officials worked in a town or village all their lives and never left it. They

△ Important officials lived in very grand houses, like the one shown by this pottery model found in a tomb.

organized the day-to-day running of their area. Archaeologists have found records on strips of bamboo that give details of the amount of grain harvested, how much was given as payment to the workers, and so on. They show that, in theory at least, the emperor's officials kept a tight hold on even the smallest detail of everyday life.

These officials and their families lived in much the same way as skilled workers and their families did. Like the craft workers, they have not left much behind for archaeologists to study. The bamboo strips that archaeologists have found were in the graves of the important officials that they were sent to.

LIVES OF THE RICH

Rich and powerful people in ancient China had beautiful homes and possessions. They had lots of servants, ate and drank well, and did not have to work. The emperor, of course, had the best of everything. We know far more about the lives of the rich, because archaeologists have found and excavated their tombs. These were full of artifacts that tell us about their lives—from pottery models of houses to the food and drink prepared for them to take to the afterlife.

Passing the time

Many rich and powerful people were supposed to rule parts of China for the emperor. In fact, their officials did all the work for them. They had to make sure that the officials worked well. Everyone from the governor down would be punished if mistakes were made. Some people took their duties seriously. Many did not. They spent all their time amusing themselves—hunting, gambling, and being entertained by acrobats, actors, and musicians.

Music for the rich

These bells were found in the tomb of the Marquis of Yi. The tomb was found in 1978 and archaeologists had to work ankle-deep in water while excavating it. The 65 bells were found still hanging on their lacquered beams, despite weighing almost 3 tons and hanging for 2,400 years. Each bell could play two notes, one when struck on the edge, the other when struck in the middle.

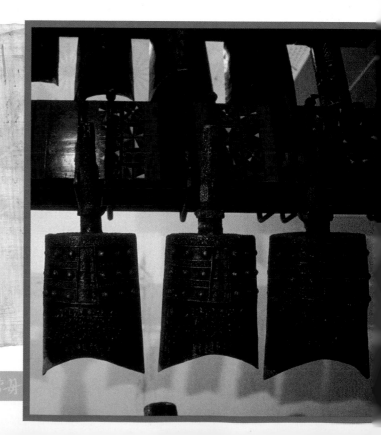

EYEWITNESS

"Although my brother is a lord, he spends all his time doing the work of his officials. A proper lord should spend his day listening to music and delighting himself with beautiful sounds."

Written by Liu Shen, son of the Emperor Jing who ruled the area around Zhongshan for his father. The brother he is talking about ruled the Zhao area.

Families

It was very important that rich and powerful men had big families. They needed sons to take over when they died. Daughters were useful, too. They could be married off into families that their father wanted to make an alliance with. This meant that unlike poorer men, rich men often married a wife and then kept several concubines—women that were not as important as the wife, but whose main job was to bring more children into the family. The emperor often had hundreds of concubines—later emperors had thousands.

Homes

The rich often had two homes, a big house in the city and an estate in the countryside. The emperor had several palaces around China, each with many buildings and beautiful gardens.

▷ *This is an artist's view of the home of a rich family.*

An important official

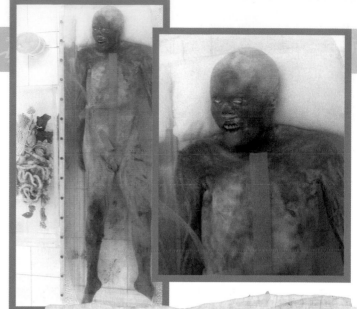

In 1975 archaeologists opened tomb 168 in Fenghuangshan, near the ancient capital city of Jinan. The tomb was built with a wooden frame to look like three rooms—a front hall, a living room and a bedroom, each with doors and windows. The body of the tomb owner was carefully laid out in the "bedroom." A collection of bamboo strips showed that the person buried in the tomb was an official of the Han Dynasty, buried in 167 B.C.E. This was confirmed by a written report in the tomb, supposedly for the ruler of the afterlife, giving the date of the funeral, the name of the dead person, where he was born, how important he was, and how many model servants had been put in his tomb. The jade seal (for sealing letters and parcels with wax) in the mouth of the corpse had the name "Sui" carved on it.

Amazingly preserved

The body of Sui Xiaoyuan was amazingly preserved, one of the best preserved bodies of an ancient Chinese person. He was about 5 feet 6 inches (1.67 meters) tall and not overweight. He was about 60 years old. His skin had not dried out or rotted, and archaeologists could move his limbs and see his fingerprints. He still had all his teeth, which were in good condition, and his body was very healthy for a man of his age.

WHO WAS Sui?

Sui Xiaoyuan was an official who ran the area for the Han Dynasty. The bamboo strips told archaeologists that he was "Wu Dai Fu"—this was level nine of a complicated system for organizing officials set up by the Han. Because we know what level he was, we also know that this means that he was paid 600 dan worth of crops a year.

Writing it down

Sui's tomb had a writing set in it. As an official, Sui spent a lot of time keeping records to show he was running his area properly. By this time people were writing with ink. Ink was made by burning different kinds of wood, coal, or even hair and bones. Fragments left on the ink grinder show that Sui's ink was made with the ash from burnt pinewood. Sui used different sized fine brushes to write on the bamboo strips. The writing set had a bronze knife in it, which he used to carefully scrape off any mistakes.

What else do we know?

Sui's tomb was filled with things he would need for the afterlife. There were wooden models of servants. There was a model boat and a chariot and horses, for traveling. There was a model stove and food. There were lots of eating, cooking, and storage pots. But we do not know if he was married or had children. Sui was buried alone. There are other tombs near by, but none that are definitely relatives, and the tomb had no clues in it about a family.

Archaeology Challenge

We know when Sui was buried, as the bamboo strips tell us. Archaeologists are not always lucky enough to find written evidence to date a burial, or any artifacts that they find. When they do not have this evidence, they use radiocarbon dating to find out how long ago a thing was made. Anything that has once been alive has a substance called Carbon 14 in it. Carbon 14 decays (disappears) away very slowly and at a rate that can be measured and is the same in anything. Archaeologists take a small sample of the artifact and measure the Carbon 14 left in it. They can date things back very accurately as far as 50,000 years ago.

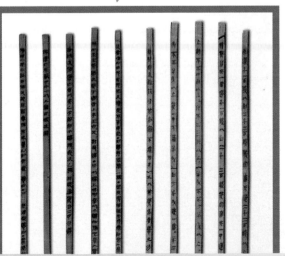

▷ *These bamboo strips provide archaeologists with a lot of information.*

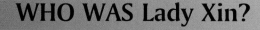
▽ *Amazingly, this silk tunic was preserved in Lady Xin's tomb.*

A rich lady's life

In 1972 archaeologists were called in to excavate a tomb site, so that a hospital could be built there. They found that it was the burial place of the Dai family. There were three tombs: one for the Lady Xin, one for her husband, and one for their son. The Lady Xin's tomb was the last and most carefully made. It was dug deep into the clay soil, surrounded with a thick layer of charcoal to soak up the moisture in the soil, and sealed tightly with more clay and rammed earth. This kept the tomb safe and preserved everything inside. There were also bamboo strips recording everything that was put into the tomb. All this gives a very clear picture of the life of a rich lady during the Han Dynasty.

WHO WAS Lady Xin?

Lady Xin was the wife of the lord of Dai, who lived during the Han dynasty. Her husband, Li Cang, ruled Changsha, in southeast China, for the Han emperors. The family burial place was near the city they had lived in, Linxiang. The Lady Xin outlived her husband and her son, and was about 50 when she died of a heart attack. Forensic scientists who examined her body found that she died suddenly, soon after eating a large piece of melon, because not all of the melon seeds had reached her stomach. Perhaps choking on one of them set off her heart attack?

Surrounded by silk

The Lady Xin was buried with a complete set of silk clothes. There were nightclothes, underwear, coats, socks, robes, skirts, gloves, slippers, and shoes. Before this archaeologists had only found a few undamaged clothes, so had to look at paintings to see exactly how people dressed.

Favorite foods

The Lady Xin clearly liked to eat. She was overweight for her age and had heart problems due to eating too much fatty food. The Chinese medicine buried with her included cinnamon, peppercorns, and the bark from a magnolia tree. These are still used in traditional Chinese medicine to treat heart disease. In her tomb there were big baskets full of eggs, plums, strawberries, dates, and pears. There were containers filled with rice, wheat, and lentils. Meats included pork, venison, beef, lamb, hare, and dog as well as chicken, goose, pheasant, sparrow, and owl. The fish, probably from the fishponds at their home, included carp, bream, perch, and mandarin fish. A container full of horsemeat, listed on the bamboo slips, had gone. Presumably one of the people filling the tomb had taken it. A lacquer tray was laid out with bowls of food for one of her favorite meals: chicken drumsticks, pork spare ribs, and fish. There were several containers of wine and tea.

△ *The musicians from the Lady Xin's tomb had their own tiny instruments. There were also several real musical instruments.*

What did she do?

Most rich ladies, like the Lady Xin, ate too much and took too little exercise. They were expected to stay at home most of the time and had servants to do all the work. There were 162 carved wooden servants in the Lady Xin's tomb. There were two larger servants that were men, probably the men who ran the house for her. The rest of the servants were women. There were also eight larger musicians and dancers. Rich women often spent a lot of time being entertained. They also liked to gamble while playing board games or, from about C.E. 900, cards.

TRAVEL AND TRADE

Most ancient Chinese people did not travel far. Road travel was uncomfortable and slow, even on the wide roads of hard-packed soil built on the orders of the First Emperor. The poor walked everywhere. The rich traveled in litters—chairs with poles on either side to carry them, or in covered wagons. They also rode horses. Government officials and messengers could use special inns built along the roads, each of them with horses to loan, so that the travelers could start the next day with a rested horse.

It was more comfortable, and quicker, to travel by water, on the rivers or around the coast of China. From the time of the First Emperor on, the ancient Chinese did everything they could to make it possible to travel as much as possible by water. They built lock gates on some rivers—gates that held water and were used to join two rivers, or parts of the same river, on different levels. They also dug out canals, man-made waterways, either to join rivers or to go in directions that rivers did not go.

Archaeology Challenge

Modern archaeologists often try to find examples of an old method of building that is still used now, so that they can study how it is done. In 1904 a western traveler wrote a description of a canal repair that used ancient Chinese techniques. Reed bundles were pushed into the hole, which was then covered with a bamboo net and held in place with bamboo rope. Bamboo rope has the same strength as a steel wire of the same size.

▷ *This is a detail from a much larger painting of the city of Kaifeng. It shows people traveling in litters, riding on horseback, and walking.*

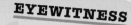

EYEWITNESS

"Nothing living was to be found, nor a drop of water; a more God-forsaken region one could not imagine on the whole Earth. Yet over 1,500 years before, a river had run where I stood."

The Swedish explorer and archaeologist Sven Hedin, talking about the Taklamakan desert in 1900.

Trade

Archaeologists know that the ancient Chinese traded with the rest of the world from very early on. The route to the west, now called the Silk Road, grew up slowly, over thousands of years. The land was more fertile in ancient times than it is now, and easier to live in and travel across. Trading was done in a series of stages, at trading places along the route.

The Silk Road

The Silk Road was not one road, but a series of linked routes that had grown up over time. By the time of the Han it stretched from Chang'an to the Mediterranean Sea and down toward India (see map below). It crossed deserts and passed through mountains, stopping at lakes and watering places. The route changed if lakes or wells dried up, and people who had lived in the towns that had grown up beside them had to move away. The Han set up forts along the way with soldiers to make sure that traders could travel safely.

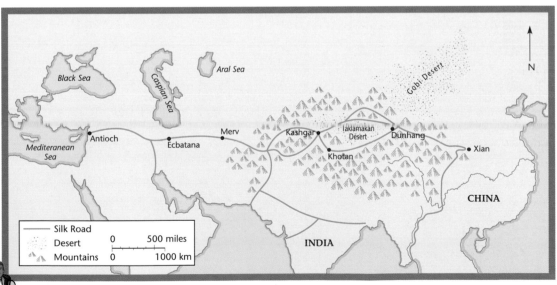

△ *The Silk Road was not just one road, but a series of trade routes that went from stopping place to stopping place.*

DID YOU KNOW? The Silk Road also had sea routes around Southeast Asia to India and beyond.

Life along the Silk Road

Archaeologists have excavated various sites along the Silk Road. These sites show that there were communities living along the paths from oasis to oasis from about 1000 B.C.E. At first routes drifted widely, as water dried up in some places and sprang up in others. But places such as Loulan and Dunhuang became established trading places, fixed points on a shifting route.

Trade on their own terms

For a long time the ancient Chinese were careful to keep China isolated from the rest of the world. They were cut off from much of the rest of the world by deserts, mountains, and the sea. The First Emperor wanted China to stay cut off, and the Great Wall sealed off the only easy way into China, from the plains to the north. From then on the Chinese kept strict control over trade and travel to and from China.

◁ *In 1994 some mummies of people who probably lived there in about 2000 B.C.E. were discovered along the Silk Road. Archaeologists were amazed that they looked more European than Asian. Their clothing, too, was in a European style.*

What did the ancient Chinese trade?

Silk was the most important thing that the Chinese traded. People all over the world wanted silk, and for thousands of years only the Chinese could make it. It was not made in the west until C.E. 1000 and, even then, the quality of Chinese silk, and the skill of Chinese weavers, meant that Chinese silk was still preferred. Ancient Roman emperors complained that so much was spent on silk that too much gold and silver was being taken out of the Roman world to the East! As trade grew under the Han and later dynasties, China also traded large amounts of fur, spices, pottery, and various items, such as mirrors, made from bronze. Many of these things have been found by archaeologists in places as far apart as India, Europe, and the Middle East.

What did the Chinese want?

Trade made China rich, but in many ways it was not something the ancient Chinese had to do. The country was so big, with such mixed weather conditions, that almost everything they needed grew, lived, or could be dug from the ground in some part of the country. Farmers grew all the food that everyone needed. So the goods that traders brought to China were almost all luxury goods. These ranged from horses (Ferghana horses were especially valuable), to linen, to foreign seeds and plants. They were also glad to have gold and silver as payment. It was not just goods that moved along the Silk Road. People brought new ideas into China, and took new ideas away, too. Chinese inventions, from silk making to ironworking methods, were carried westwards.

△ *Camels were vital for transporting goods along the Silk Road. They could go for long periods without water, while still carrying heavy loads.*

DID YOU KNOW? Buddhism came to China from India.

INVENTIONS

The ancient Chinese invented many of the things we now use every day. Many were invented during the Tang and Song Dynasties. When you write a letter, help in the garden, or go to a firework party you use one of their inventions. Some of these inventions were passed along to other people, often on trade routes. Some of them other people had to discover all over again. Here are just a few.

The magnetic compass

The magnetic compass was the first really reliable way to work out direction when you were out at sea, out of sight of land. It was invented by the ancient Chinese. The idea of a magnetic compass used on land, called a "south pointer," was being written about as early as 350 B.C.E. The first reference we have to one being used at sea is in C.E. 1119.

Paper

Before the invention of paper, the ancient Chinese either wrote on silk (which was expensive) or on bamboo strips (which had little space and were best for lists). What they wanted was something that was cheap and long lasting. First, they experimented with the stalks of the hemp plant. Archaeologists found a scrap of this kind of paper in a Han grave. It was made in about 100 B.C.E. and was quite thick. Writing from the time suggests that this paper was used not to write on, but for hankies, as packaging, or oiled and used to make raincoats or umbrellas. Mixing the hemp with bark and rags made a thinner paper. By C.E. 100 paper was being used for letters and official documents.

The wheelbarrow

Stories from ancient China tell of a man who built himself "a wooden goat or sheep" to carry things in around 100 B.C.E. The first evidence of a wheelbarrow to be found by archaeologists is in a carving of the wall of a Han tomb, which shows a man pushing a wheelbarrow.

The rudder

A rudder is like a long oar that is fixed to the back of a ship to help to steer it. Archaeologists have found several models of ships in Han tombs that have rudders. The ancient Chinese were well ahead of the West in boat design. The Guangzhou shipyards from late in the First Emperor's reign could work with ships 262 feet (80 meters) long and 98 feet (30 meters) wide. The *Mayflower*, built to take settlers from Britain to America in 1620 was 60 feet (18 meters) long and 26 feet (8 meters) wide.

Fireworks

The ancient Chinese invented gunpowder by accident in about C.E. 850. By about C.E. 900 they were using it in war. By about C.E. 1050 they were using gunpowder to make a whole range of fireworks, using different chemicals, metals, and ground rock to make different colours. "Water rats" were fireworks fixed on tiny skis to shoot across the water. "Ground rats" did the same on wheels on land.

The first plane?

While China was divided after the end of the Han dynasty, part of northern China was ruled by the Qi dynasty. The first Qi emperor executed families that rebelled against him by making them "fly" from a high tower with wings made from bamboo mats.

ARCHAEOLOGY IN MODERN CHINA

Many Chinese archaeologists work permanently at the terracotta warriors site, near Xian. The site is a World Heritage site and draws visitors from all over the world, all through the year. The site needs all kinds of archaeologists—people to excavate the huge areas that are still untouched, people to piece together the shattered warriors, and people to preserve the finds. Archaeologists who work here are likely to have access to the most modern techniques. However, more small-scale excavations are going on all over the country.

What is HEMA?

HEMA is a chemical that archaeologists are using to preserve the colored lacquer on the terracotta warriors as they are excavated. The first warriors to be found had color on them, too, but much of it flaked away over time once they were exposed to the air. The warriors are coated in HEMA as soon as the earth has been cleared off them. An electric beam is then passed all over them, which seals the color from the air that would dry it out and cause it to flake off.

▷ *While these archaeologists carefully work to excavate the warriors, some work to preserve them, and scientists try to find out more about how they were made.*

42

Early brain surgery

In June 2001 archaeologists were examining a 5,000-year-old skull when they noticed a small hole in the back of the skull. The used a computer to make 3D images of the skull and also enlarged and enhanced the picture on computer. There were also scratch marks made by tools. Professor Bao Xiufeng, a surgeon, said they were from surgery while the patient was still alive, and there was some bone regrowth, to suggest the patient survived the operation.

△ *There are still many finds being made in China by archaeologists today.*

Finds large and small

All kinds of finds can open a window on ancient Chinese life. In July 2002 archaeologists discovered 20,000 bamboo slips in Hunan province, dating from 770 B.C.E. to C.E. 25. Only 2,000 slips were found in the last century, so archaeologists are comparing the importance of this discovery to the discovery of the terracotta warriors. They will take many years to transcribe and read. On the other hand, a single letter found in the Xuanquanzhi Ruins near Dunhuang in northwest China, tells us a great deal, too. It was written on silk during the Han Dynasty. The writer lived on the western borders of China and the letter was being sent to a friend further inland. It shows that there was a post office at Dunhuang, part of a system that archaeologists think ran all along the Silk Road. The writer says life is hard on the border, and there are many things he needs. He wants his friend to buy him some supplies and send them to Dunghang, where he will have them collected.

Ancient China's history is divided up into dynasties. These are chunks of time when one particular family ruled China. There were several periods of unrest and civil war, when a dynasty could not keep control of the whole country. At these times the country was broken up into kingdoms that fought among themselves until one was strong enough to take over the others and start a new dynasty.

2205–1818 B.C.E.
Possible Xia Dynasty
2000 City of Erlitou built.

1500–1050 B.C.E.
Shang Dynasty
1500 First writing we are able to read.

1050–475 B.C.E.
Zhou Dynasty

475–221 B.C.E.
Warring States Period
China broke up into many different states, each governed by a warlord. These states were often at war, although they also made groups of alliances against other states. Then the state of Qin gradually took over more and more of the other states until China was united again under the Qin Dynasty.

221–207 B.C.E.
Qin Dynasty
China is united by the First Emperor, Shihuangdi.
Great Wall is built across China's northern border.

206 B.C.E.–C.E. 220
Han Dynasty
C.E. 23–25
There was a two year civil war that broke up the Han dynasty. To separate the two periods of Han rule, the first is called the Western Han and the second is called the Eastern Han. These names come from the different parts of the country that each group ruled from.

C.E. 220–589
The last Han ruler, Xiandi, could not keep control. China broke up into three kingdoms which broke up into smaller kingdoms in C.E. 265.

C.E. 581 618
Sui Dynasty
China is reunited by Wendi who encouraged the spread of Buddhism in China. His son Yangdi built the Grand Canal that joined two of China's great rivers: the Yellow River and the Yangtze River.

C.E. 618–907
Tang Dynasty
The second Tang emperor, Taizong (626-648), had had a lot of success as an army leader under his father. As emperor he showed that he was also clever and good at choosing people to work for him. He worked as hard as his officials and was fair to his people.

The third Tang ruler, Gaozong (649-683) was a weak man and in his rule China was really run, for the first time, by a woman, his wife, Wu Zetian. She ran China until her death in 705.

C.E. 907–960
In C.E. 907 the advisor who had really been ruling China for the last thirty years took power for himself. This broke China up again into several warring kingdoms, as other families refused to accept his rule.

C.E. 960–1279
Song Dynasty
In C.E. 1126 it looked as if the Song Dynasty would die out. But a Song prince managed to regain control. Because he carried on the Song Dynasty while ruling from a capital city in the south of China, the Song period is divided up into Northern Song (until he began to rule) and Southern Song (after he began to rule).

C.E. 1279
In C.E. 1279 Mongols from the north invaded and captured China.

TIMELINE OF ARCHAEOLOGY

170

Sima Qian writes Records of a Historian.

1899

First oracle bones found.

1900

The Swedish explorer, Sven Hedin, discovers the ancient city of Loulanin in the deserts along the Silk Road.

1907

Aurel Stein visits caves at Dunghang. He takes 29 boxes of Buddhist scrolls back to Britain. He sets off a rush of people to Dunhuang to find more.

1922

Carl Whiting Bishop leads his first expedition to China for the Freer Gallery.

1928

Shang city of Anyang found. From this time up to the present day there have been almost continuous excavations.

1949

People's Republic of China set up. Makes it hard for westerners to take artifacts out of China and to enter China to excavate. But takes control of archaeology and funds excavations.

1954

Earliest iron-making factory discovered at Xinglong, Hubei province. It dates back to the Warring States period.

1959

Earliest ancient Chinese city, Erlitou, found. Dispute over whether it is from the Xia or the Shang period.

1968

Tomb of Liu Sheng and one of his wives (Dou Wan) discovered on Mount Ling. They were both wearing jade suits that covered the whole body, even their heads.

1972

Tombs of the Lady Xin, her husband Li Cong, and their son discovered.

1974

First Emperor's terracotta warriors discovered, by farmers digging a well at Xi Yang.

1975

Tomb of Sui Xiaoyuan found in Fenghuangshan, near Jinan. Sui's body had been amazingly well preserved.

1976

Tomb of Fu Hao, wife of the Shang emperor Wu Ding, discovered at Anyang.

1986

Pits at Sanxingdui found, shows there were people other than the Shang in China who were setting up cities.

2001

Discovery of a Chinese skull about 5,000 years old that had had brain surgery.

2002

About 20,000 bamboo slips found in Hunan province dating between 770 B.C.E. and C.E. 25. It will take years to transcribe and read them all.

anthropology
study of human origins, societies, and cultures

archaeologist
person who studies the past by examining and scientifically analyzing old objects and ruins

archer
person who shoots with a bow and arrow

artifact
object made by people, such as a tool or ornament. Archaeologists often use the word "artifact" to describe an object they find that was made by people in past times.

Bodhisattva Guanyin
Chinese Buddhist goddess of mercy. When Buddhism first came to China this god was male. A Chinese empress changed it to female.

burial pit
hole dug deep into the ground where people are buried, often with possessions for the afterlife

capital city
most important town or city in the country or region

cavalry
soldiers who fight on horseback

charioteer
soldier who drives a chariot, a two-wheeled horse-drawn vehicle

clan
large group of families, all related to each other in some way, perhaps only by a shared relative in the distant past

communal
shared or done by members of a community

concubine
woman who lives with the emperor, but is not his wife. A concubine was expected to produce children, but was not as important as the emperor's wife.

conscript
somebody called up for compulsory military service

court
residence, councillors, and household staff of the emperor

dan
ancient Chinese unit of money related to how much grain could be grown on a piece of land

Daoism
following the teachings of Lao Tzu

dynasty
succession of rulers from the same family

forensic scientist
somebody who scientifically analyses human remains and other evidence

kingdom
country ruled by a single ruler, usually called a king

lacquer
varnish made from the sap of an Asian tree

litter
big roofed bed with curtains all around and poles on each side so it could be carried

lock gate
moveable gate used to dam a small section of canal or river so that boats can be raised or lowered by changing the level of the water

loot
to break into a place, steal from it, and wreck it

Marquis
nobleman from an important family, often rich as well as important

mass produced
items made in large numbers, at the same time, in the same way

medieval
another word for the Middle Ages. Different people give different start and end dates for this period, depending on what they are studying. The widest range is C.E. 600–1500.

meditate
when somebody relaxes and thinks carefully about their life

millet
cereal crop with small seeds, used to make flour

Mongol
person from Mongolia

officer
person holding a position of authority in the army

official
person holding a position of authority in a government organization

People's Republic of China
full name of China since 1949

pottery

things made from clay

radiocarbon dating

way of discovering the age of some objects by measuring the amount of substance, called carbon, that they contain. It works because plants and animals absorb a special type of carbon, Carbon-14, from the air when they are alive. When they die, this carbon disappears at a known rate. So the amount present in a piece of wood, bone, or other material that was once a part of a plant or animal reveals how old the material is.

settlement

somewhere that a group of people build homes to live and work together

Silk Road

name given to the various trade routes that ran from China to the West

tax

money or items (such as crops) paid to the state by individuals from their earnings

terraced

area of hillside with a series of flat areas, like steps, used for growing plants and crops

terracotta

baked clay

tomb

structure where someone is buried

trade route

road or sea crossing that traders always follow from their home to the place they are trading with

Warring States period

period following the Shang Dynasty (1500–1050 B.C.E) and before the Qin Dynasty (221–207 B.C.E) when China was not ruled by a single emperor, but broke up into several states that were almost always at war

FURTHER READING

Minnis, Ivan. *You Are in Ancient China*. Chicago: Raintree, 2004.

Shuter, Jane. *Ancient Chinese Art*. Chicago: Heinemann Library, 2001.

Waterlow, Julia. *The Ancient Chinese*. New York: Thompson Learning, 1994.